MAVENS, MENTORS
AND MASTERS OF THE UNIVERSE
IN THE DIGITAL AGE

Howard Tullman

Published in the United States of America
For bulk orders, please contact info@blogintobook.com

Cover design portrait courtesy of Matthew Cherry
Perspiration Principles logo designed by James "Red" Schmitt
Special Thanks to Lakshmi Shenoy and Claudia Saric

To purchase all volumes of The Perspiration Principles, please visit:
BlogIntoBook.com/tullman/

ISBN: 9781619849808

DEDICATION

Sitting down every week to write something that will be meaningful and ideally of lasting value to others is a lot like setting out to start a new business. Sometimes there's a germ of an idea; sometimes it's an emotional reaction or other driver; or perhaps it's just a problem or situation that needs to be addressed. And occasionally you simply want to see things change and no one else is stepping up to the plate to make that happen.

You can't know how hard, long or costly (in many ways) the journey will be and there are no guarantees that anything good will ever come of your efforts, but you know for certain that nothing will ever happen if you don't get the process started and try. It's a lonely path and every bit of encouragement, assistance and support that you find along the way makes the job a little easier and slightly more likely to succeed.

I hope that these books will be my modest contribution to your success and to the well-worn and tattered bag of hopes and dreams which we call entrepreneurship.

CONTENTS

WHEN YOU COME TO
THE FORK, TAKE IT

W e've been told practically since birth that a lot of the success we hope for in business (and in life) will come from being a good listener and from being <u>really</u> good at following directions. Consistency is another highly regarded and very traditional virtue along with learning from our experiences. But what if - in a world driven and dominated by technology that is changing much faster than ever before and picking up more speed every day – all of this conventional wisdom was basically wrong?

What if past experience wasn't your best friend, but your worst enemy because it was no longer predictive of virtually anything and, worse yet, because it was actually an impediment to the kinds of disruptive change and innovation that we need today to remain competitive and ultimately to lead the global pack? Letting go of what has worked for you in the past isn't ever easy, but it's ever more critical that these kinds of questions be a significant part of the decision set.

What if being consistent wasn't the smart thing to do (that is – to keep doing things the way you had always done them), but was actually fairly stupid in that it meant that - in the months and years that had intervened since you initially made a plan and started executing it – you hadn't learned anything that required changes, updates, pivots or even dropping whole lines of unproductive or unprofitable business? As Emerson said, "a foolish consistency is the hobgoblin of little minds." And frankly, who really needs more hobgoblins – whatever they are?

I'm especially concerned these days about a different kind of directions (in the compass sense of the word (North or South – to or from) rather than meaning "instructions") and how important it is going to be for all of us to understand and appreciate the ways in which the flows of critical information, assets and resources have reversed their directions/polarities over the last few years so that we can quickly adapt our businesses and our operations to address the new and very different requirements that these changes dictate. And to understand the necessary changes, we're going to need some very smart people and some strong compasses (rather than historical road maps which aren't worth much these days) to help us find our way.

What's the absolutely simplest example? The obvious fact that ubiquitous connectivity, information sharing and universal access have turned every form of publication, broadcast and communication (formerly one-way or one-to-many) into a bi-directional or multi-directional conversation (at least two-way or more). The "I talk, you listen" model of anything (media, sales and marketing, education and training, and even governance) is totally toast. Everyone's an "expert"; every opinion (based on facts or factoids) registers and counts; and sadly, in many cases, the biggest blowhard beats the brightest bulb. Sheer tonnage today trumps tact and very often the truth. This situation can't last, but it's what we've got to deal with today. The goal is to find the new business opportunities and advantages hidden in the piles of gossip and garbage.

And what does the omnipresent cloud and the massive amounts of content of all kinds which now reside there tell us about the changed directions? It tells us that we're entering a world of PULL where we'll pull (and extract) information and intelligence from the cloud as and when needed and where we're in control of the information equation rather than PUSH (and swallow) where we're simply passive consumers of whatever crap is forced down the pipelines and feed to us. There's just too much noise, too much information, and too many complex and overwhelming decisions coming at us for anyone to effectively process the data and make wise choices.

But that's exactly the kind of information overload that makes for great opportunities for those companies which can help us choose, niche, filter, process and decide what makes sense for each of us. Companies that can help us find just what we're looking for (and no more) will set the standards for search in the future because "knowing" is going to be an insurmountable task for anyone whereas "knowing where to look" to find the answers will be the new name of the game. Chicago-based SimpleRelevance (www. simplerelevance.com) is a start-up developing and providing cost-effective analytical tools for the "rest of us" to make smart choices and sense out of masses of available (but not necessarily readily accessible) data in a cost-effective manner.

The truth is that – in virtually every commercial exchange – the information equation has been reversed because of the improved access (for better or worse) which buyers have to group intelligence, shared opinion and pricing data which were formerly held and controlled solely by sellers and the playing field for negotiations has been altered in the consumers' favor forever. And this isn't simply a matter of getting a better price on some product or selecting a smarter service provider for your lawn care.

It's clear that no industry or profession is immune to these directional shifts. Medicine offers two great examples. First, in the old days, we picked a doctor (usually through family connections or other word of mouth) and then – if necessary – the doctor told us which hospital he or she was connected with and that's where we went for our surgery or other procedures. There was no choice, no shopping around, no arguing – just "doctor's orders". In the near future, that order will be completely reversed for the vast majority of patients in America. We will pick or be assigned a health services organization and that company will specify and dictate our hospital, our doctor, and even to a very large extent our course of treatment or non-treatment. Accountants and clerks we've never met will decide whether we "need" (and their companies will pay for) certain tests and medication rather than our doctors.

And if these changes didn't make our doctors feel somewhat diminished (to say the least), just think about how drug advertising has changed the game and turned them into glorified waiters and order takers. In the grand old days, if we were sick and saw our doctor, he prescribed any necessary medications. In fact, that ability – to write scripts - was the defining legal characteristic of being a doctor. Today, thanks to TV and the web, we go into the doctor's office and tell him that we need the "purple pill" or a Z-pack and we won't take "no" for an answer because we saw it on TV and now we're the experts. Talk about TMI. And, as a result, the doctors spend their days arguing with us about ads we've seen on the tube rather than telling us what we need (or very often) or don't need for our problems. And if we don't like their answer or their reluctance to give us what we think we need, increasingly, we can go to see a nurse practitioner or clerk at our neighborhood drug store and get our fix right there.

As the information around us expands and implodes at the same time, and we are all swamped in the unceasing flow of data and TMI, we're looking at another major inflection point (or - as Yogi Berra would say – another fork in the road) and, while it's not very clear what lies on the path ahead, it's obvious that if we don't make some hard choices and just stand still, we'll be run over. Where you head is less important today than the fact that you keep moving and head somewhere. When you get to the fork in the road, take it.

SHUT UP AND LISTEN - YOU MIGHT JUST LEARN SOMETHING

One of the most interesting parts of my job at 1871 is listening to our member companies. For most entrepreneurs, effective and patient listening is a fairly foreign concept. They think that the opposite of talking isn't listening; it's waiting to talk. Partially this is because they think that they have to always be selling and they're always trying to fill any dead air and suck all the oxygen out of the room. But sometimes, you just need to catch your breath and let the other guy have his say. As it happens, bits of actual wisdom are the rewards you often get for listening when you would have preferred to speak.

These days, I think that listening is a rare and highly undervalued skill. It's an area in which everyone of us could use some improvement and developing good listening skills can make a world of difference for your business and in your leadership. Listening carefully is the highest form of courtesy and professionalism. As my Mother used to say: "this is why God gave us two ears and only one mouth." If I had only listened back then, there's no telling where I'd be today.

So every day I get to hear as much and as many of the trials and tribulations of the hundreds of entrepreneurs who work here at startup central as I can stand. I try to be patient and objective as long as they have taken the time: (1) to do their homework and get prepared; (2) to organize their thoughts and their questions; and (3) to specifically identify the areas where they think I can help or at least advise them. Folks who just drop by to shoot the breeze quickly find themselves shooting it somewhere else with someone else.

If they're not prepared and if they have that little respect for my time; it's hard to imagine that they would really care about my thoughts and opinions or that I should waste my relatively scarce time sharing my reactions with them. I think this is a very fair expectation on both sides of the discussion – whether you're the "oldie" or the "newbie" in any conversation; you need to bring it or don't bother coming.

And, of course in the course of the conversations, generally when I'm asked, and often whether or not I'm asked, I'm not especially shy (and rarely polite) about giving them my impressions and the alleged benefit of my years of experience which may occasionally keep them from making the same mistakes that I made in similar circumstances. Sometimes, I discover that they're trying to create solutions before they've spent enough time listening to their customers' problems which is a lot like working in the dark. Other times I find that just the act of having someone seriously listening to them (who doesn't have an attitude, an interest or an agenda) does wonders for their mental health and their anxiety levels. But that's not to say that I think that these skull sessions should be warm and fuzzy chats.

I like to save the "strokes" for their co-workers, friends and families. Honestly, I'd rather be fair and frank than spend my time beating around the bush and worrying more about their feelings than their future. My process is aggressive and unapologetic – I'm trying to make them and their businesses better – that's all there is to it. It's never about me. But it does have a lot to do with argument and challenge – pressing and pushing them to think about the tough issues and the non-obvious answers - rather than supplying their standard responses. I want to make sure that they have the courage of their convictions and the willingness to stick by their guns. We often describe this posture as "sometimes wrong, but never in doubt."

That's because you need a thick skin to succeed in this crazy startup business and the internal and external calluses which will ultimately come to protect you are developed and grow strong in the crucible of confrontation (and hard questions) and not in courteous conversations steeped in superficial compliments. Some babies are just ugly – and some ideas just suck. It always helps to tell it like it is and the truth only hurts when it should.

Having said all that, I'd still certainly rather have them not just listen to my advice, but take it as well. I do vehemently believe that great serial entrepreneurs are masters in pattern recognition and – in the startup space – there are very, very few problems and very little else that represent truly new issues or – as the courts say – cases of first impression. In 95% of the situations, for better or worse, these are "movies" that I've seen before. Everyone I know and those I speak to about this who have made it their life's work to consistently light up new businesses will tell you that – while you're always gonna make new mistakes – the real key to succeeding more often than you fail is to avoid making the same mistakes over and over again.

I can't speak for the many guys who've been successful once in this business of new businesses – I'm sure that even they aren't sure whether they were terribly smart or terrifically lucky or, most likely, a bunch of both. It's never really that clear whether their particular success was mainly due to a good idea, good partners, good timing or simple good luck – not that there's anything wrong with any of these elements. I like to say: "Just because you've done it once doesn't make you Jesus."

And I've written before about marginal mentors (http://www.inc.com/howard-tullman/how-to-deal-with-marginal-mentors.html) and on the subject of how little having made or accumulated a lot of money has to do with having the mental horsepower and the chops to help someone drag his business out of a ditch. Money doesn't really care who makes it and having a lot of money – as we all know from experience – clearly doesn't make you wise.

But for those of us who have lived through the very prolonged and painful process of successfully birthing businesses over and over again, it all comes down to listening and paying attention. And to one more important thing: the winners are those who learn to listen patiently without losing either their self-confidence or their temper.

DO MARGINAL MENTORS
REALLY MATTER?

I'm fairly certain that there's an overabundance of highly-verbal and successful people who are flattered to be asked and more than willing and even excited about the prospect of giving sporadic advice to young entrepreneurs. I say "sporadic" because - even in the best and most structured and organized incubators, accelerators and other start-up and tune-up support facilities - the mentoring process has a lot of hit and miss qualities. People drop by for an hour or two – rarely actually up-to-speed on the business in question or the critical issues on the table – and then they listen briefly to the entrepreneurs, nod sagely, take their best shot at some quick suggestions and advice and then leave. And sadly, the next guy dropping in to meet with that same team might have identical or completely opposite advice.

It's no doubt a learning experience for the entrepreneurs, but I'm not really sure what they're learning or gaining from the process. I believe that when you take the time to give someone advice (and you take their time as well), you're obligated to do what you can (in terms of preparation, connections, referrals, etc.) to make sure that it's not just lip service or a bunch of empty clichés.

Some of these "advisors" are one-hit wonders themselves and it's not really that clear whether their particular success was mainly due to a good idea, good partners, good timing or simple good luck – not that there's anything wrong with any of these elements – and I'd rather be blessed in any business with all of the above if I had a choice. But you have to wonder – as you're listening to their war stories – exactly how much transferable wisdom they've gained from the experience and, more specifically, how much they've extracted and generalized from their situation which will be of use and value to your own business.

Giving advice is a form of high-minded, self-congratulatory nostalgia for these folks in many respects and, in addition, it's frightfully easy in these situations to tell someone else what to do because nothing is impossible for the person who doesn't have to do it himself. What's more, a lot of these people will tell you to take a hard line on something and stand up on principle until push comes to shove and then they're long gone. I like to say that a principle really isn't a principle until it costs you something.

Another aspect of the process that's somewhat problematic is the matter of money. Money doesn't care who makes it and having a lot of money – as we all know from experience – doesn't really make you wise or make you a class act. And I realize that rich entrepreneurs sometimes complain that when you have money, people tend to doubt your talent. But in many cases that's exactly the fact. And, for me, it's really hard to pay a lot of attention to the advice of someone with no skin in the game. I like people who put their money where their mouth is. My favorite trader (I realize that's somewhat of an oxymoron) likes to say that "until you have a position, all you have is an opinion" and I agree.

Any entrepreneur's time is precious and constrained – if you're going to spend it listening to anyone for any substantial amount of time, make sure (as best you can) that they know what they're talking about and that the conversations are worth your time.

Here are a couple of thoughts to help you through the process.

(1) As Simon and Garfunkel said so well in *The Boxer:* "…a man hears what he wants to hear/and disregards the rest". Listen carefully, weigh everything with a grain of salt, and try to determine why the person would (or should) know what they're talking about. Then take the best and leave the rest.

(2) If the person is also a prospective investor in your business (and one that you think you'd like to have and could live with), remember that listening to advice very often accomplishes far more than actually heeding it. Be patient, nod your head a lot, agree with their observations, and then go on and do what you think is best for the business. Frankly, I think in crazy times like these, lying probably gets more businesses started than money.

(3) Try to remember that personality and rapport are not substitutes for credibility and knowledge. They make for pleasant conversations, but just because someone's a really good guy only rarely also means that he knows what he's talking about. These are people you'd happily buy a drink for, but never lend any money.

And finally, keep in mind the strange paradox that there are people who can give you extremely useful and valuable information and direction, but who can't get out of their own way in their own businesses and who would be the first to admit that they really don't do a good job of taking their own advice. Don't follow their example, but listen to their suggestions.

SHOULD EVERY "EXPERT" COMES WITH AN EXPIRATION DATE

These days, for better or worse, professed experts in every conceivable area of business are a dime a dozen and, in most cases, I'd say that they (and their alleged expertise and invaluable advice) are worth just about that much. And, in all events, they are clearly worth considerably less than you'd spend on a good cup of coffee. And just like spoiled cream can kill a great cup of java; out-of-date ideas from people who the developments in new technologies have clearly passed by should be date-stamped with the understanding that their time has come and gone and that they're no longer worth listening to – politely or otherwise.

It seems that everyone claims to be an expert on something today and they're shameless and more than happy to sell you (and everyone you know) their various services for a tidy sum. Some of these people are one-hit wonders trying to re-invent themselves and it's not clear whether their prior "success" was mainly due to a good idea, good partners, good timing or simple good luck. So you have to wonder – as you're listening to their war stories – exactly how much transferable wisdom they've gained from their own experiences and how much of that knowledge will be of use and value to your own business.

And, just like cigarettes, I think a lot of these characters ought to come with a large warning label (maybe something like "take this advice with as many large grains of salt as possible") because – in addition to wasting your time and money – these people can be clearly be harmful to your business. And their misdirected guidance can take years off your life - just like a pack-a-day smoking habit. In today's high-velocity and hyper-competitive markets; speed kills (in a good way) if it's you that's moving down the road. But if you're heading in the wrong direction because you listened to the wrong advice; you could find yourself way behind the curve and trying to play catch-up with your competition.

Now, I'm sure there are always valuable things to be learned from others and that - within their own experience base and their given areas of expertise – there really are experts who can add value to your strategy and your business if their input is timely and current. But it's not easy to separate the wheat from the chaff or to figure out who can really give you a helping hand and your money's worth. Your time is a scarce and precious resource and it's always constrained. If you're going to spend it listening to anyone for any substantial amount of time, make sure (as best you can) that they know what they're talking about and that the conversations are worth it.

I think that there are a few guidelines and ideas to keep in mind when you find yourself having to evaluate situations like this.

(1) Process Experts Have a Longer Shelf Life than Domain Experts

A domain expert knows a lot about what to do in a specific area or situation and in a defined space or industry. That knowledge is the stuff that spoils quickly over time if it's not refreshed and renewed – especially with regard to new technologies. It's critical to be a life-long and continual learner. A process expert knows how to repeatedly do things effectively in whatever situation or industry you happen to be in. Successful serial entrepreneurs call this skill "pattern recognition" and it means simply that many situations present problems that aren't materially different (regardless of the specifics) from those that seasoned operators have seen and solved hundreds of times before. Guys who know the proper approaches and have mastered the change management process never go out of date.

(2) An Expert's Knowledge Can Exceed His Experience But Only Rarely

There's a lot of delusional mythology around the extensibility of skills and expertise. Much of this BS is promulgated by the people trying to sell you their services even when it's an obvious stretch and a complete leap of faith to believe that they can really add value based on their actual backgrounds and experience. Even the most successful players need to know and – more importantly – admit the limits of their skill sets. You only need to recall Michael Jordan's abortive career as a professional baseball player to see what I'm sayin'. Lawyers (as a race) are also great at never saying "No" to doing anything regardless of their actual qualifications. They're always ready to take the fee and the assignment and then you have the privilege (and the risks) of paying for their OTJ learning curve and education. Not a smart choice – ever. You need to find the right person with the right experience and tools in the right industry (your industry) and not try to make do or accept someone saying that what they did elsewhere is easy to apply to your situation.

(3) Knowledge is Subject to the Law of Diminishing Returns in Most Cases

In addition to simply going stale or out of date, whatever accumulation of knowledge and expertise you may have and apply to your situation, you should understand that it can only take you so far. It's true that we are always learning, but that doesn't mean that we are necessarily getting smarter in the process. After a certain point, the facts and figures and past wisdom run out of steam and this is when the best entrepreneurs really earn their stripes and their keep. It's at the point when you need to use your best judgment; your intuition; and a little prayer (which never hurts) to get you over the last hurdle and through the woods to the finish line that you learn whether you've got what it takes to succeed. No one else can do it for you. No one else can make those last calls and choices. It's all up to you because – in the final analysis – and in the critical moments of decision – no one knows your business better than you.

(4) Hire the Expert Who Can Get You There, not the One Who Says He's Been There Before

In business, just as in your sex life, especially as you get older, it's important to remember that past results are no guarantee of future performance. A track record is an important and very valuable part of the evaluation process for any expert, but you're not headed backwards and your job is to make sure that the people you are planning to work with have the desire, the energy and the skills to help you move your business forward.

DEALING WITH DOOFUSES AND OTHER WASTES OF TIME

I like to think that the best entrepreneurs are masters of cutting to the chase. They're very focused, of course, but more importantly they're especially efficient because they don't really have any other choice. Scarce resources, limited time, and a regularly shrinking bank account do a whole lot for your concentration. And the non-stop streams of decisions (large and small) which they face every day are roughly like living in a batting cage with a machine firing fastball pitches at your head every 15 seconds. It means they've got to be 'on purpose" and "on point" all the time. Patience isn't exactly a virtue in this kind of frantic fast-forward environment and tolerance – especially of time-wasting doofuses – is a very rare commodity.

In addition, because entrepreneurs live in a world where they need to be constantly calculating opportunity costs, the smartest ones are always asking themselves the same two questions:

(1) Is what I'm doing right now moving us forward toward the goal; and

(2) Is what I'm doing right now the highest and best use of my time and talents?

Frankly, if you're not asking yourselves these same questions at least a couple of times a day, then your people and your business are running your life and making your choices for you instead of the other way around which is how it should be. You always want to run the business based on your outbox and not your inbox.

It's absolutely true that (starting with Steve Jobs) some of the sharpest and most effective CEOs I have known over the last 30 years might seem like arrogant, asocial and abrupt assholes to most people (and that's when they're in a good mood), but, in their hearts (or what's left of them), they're just aggressively optimizing their time and their opportunities on a continual basis and constantly assigning new priorities to things in real time. They aren't being rude or dismissive; they're just attentive to things that they regard at that moment as more important. They're doing what they think is right – right at that moment – no more, no less and no promises as to what the next moment will bring. That's just how it works.

To say that they don't suffer fools lightly is a gross understatement. The truth is that they regard most people as something between a nuisance and a necessary evil. But the fact is that we need leaders like this to make important things happen and they can't all be charming social butterflies even if they had the time which, of course, they don't. As the old saying goes: "money doesn't come from singing. It comes from work."

So it usually falls to other people in the organization to help the fiercely focused founders and CEOs figure out how to deal with the people who are simply doofuses, masters of make-work, and/ or wizards of window-dressing and who, for better or worse (and mainly for worse), are not only necessary evils; they're generally part of the whole package that comes with your decision to accept third-party financing whether it's high-end angel investors, private equity groups or traditional venture investors.

If you take their money, you get to take all the crap that comes right along with it and you're supposed to smile at that prospect. Thank you, sir. May I have another? But, smiling or shrugging (just don't get caught sulking), every entrepreneur needs to figure out how to deal with these people because they're here to stay. It's not easy (it's a little like putting out a fire in your hair with a hammer), but it does help to understand who you're dealing with and how you can help. Frankly, anything that you can do as a senior team member to help your fiercely focused CEO manage this process and also to run interference for the rest of the folks on the team couldn't be more valuable.

First, and foremost, remember who you're going to actually be dealing with from day-to-day.

I guess there's a version of the old "bait and switch" routine in every business – the car guys may be the masters, but the VCs and PE guys aren't very far behind in the BS business. You start out talking to a guy who could buy a small country and end up working with people who can't approve a pepperoni pizza for a party without checking with personnel. It's a rude awakening and disappointing for sure – but it's just another part of the business that you need to get used to. The trick is to get the rules of engagement straight at the outset and to not let the turkeys get you down.

Second, you need to remember that these folks basically have never begun or run anything.

By and large, you'll learn that they are consumed with matters and minutia of form over substance. They worry much more about font sizes and folders than about the actual facts and figures of the business. It's all about presentations and the "process" rather than real prospects and progress. None of these guys wants to give their

Emperor(s) the bad news. I call this the doctrine of "no <u>new</u> news is ever good news". Their absolute worst nightmare is to EVER be the bearer of changes, surprises or any bad news. They know only too well what happens to the messenger.

<u>Third</u>, generally the players that you're unlucky enough to get stuck with really don't have day jobs.

As far as I can tell, their main occupation (other than making work for you) is to somehow justify their own positions. They can turn the simple scheduling of meetings (the more the merrier) into major undertakings and marathons of telephone and email tag. And they think the meetings themselves are the end game and that counting meetings counts – rather than what gets done in the meetings. And it gets worse. Everything they touch has to be over-analyzed; repeatedly chewed over; and ultimately cleared with everyone including the dog in the lobby. It's a painful, time-wasting process.

<u>Finally</u>, I really wasn't kidding about the pizza. These people have absolutely no ultimate authority to do or approve anything (other than hiring outside consultants on your dime) without running back and clearing it with a multitude of higher-ups. The only way that you can ever lose your job at one of these investment firms is by saying "yes" to something. No one ever lost their job by saying "no" and that's not going to change in our lifetimes. So it's pretty much a waste of your time and your breath to ask these guys for anything since they can't write the check in any event. You don't want to be dealing with the monkey when the organ grinder is in the room.

So, what can you do to keep things moving forward for the business in spite of these people?

(1) You can't completely ignore them, but you can take your time in responding and this will actually save you time and

effort in the long run because – as often as not – they'll never follow up and pursue many of their demands.

(2) You can do whatever you can to contain and limit their involvement (and thereby protect at least some of your team's time) by insisting on being the funnel for all their interactions with and inquiries to the team.

(3) As a test, you can initially respond to certain requests simply and quickly and then determine whether anyone is actually reading, reviewing and/or acting upon any of the submitted materials. Much of the time you'll never hear another word on the subject because it's likely that no one will even be looking at the stuff requested.

(4) But, sadly, here's the one thing you can't do: you actually can't try to go around these mini-gatekeepers in order to try to get to the real decision makers because – just like in any classic John le Carre espionage novel – it turns out that everyone on their side (top to bottom) is a part of the program and needs to preserve the fiction that their plans, processes and procedures actually make sense and work. No one, including the Emperor, wants to ever hear otherwise.

SITUATIONAL ETHICS SUCK

I'm afraid that we're developing another generation gap and this one isn't merely cosmetic (can't stand those tattoos!) or aurally aesthetic (can't stand that music!) or even extreme economic (why "own" anything). It's far more important than any of these fairly superficial differences and preferences – albeit I recognize that they are crushingly important to the hosts of *TMZ* and *Access Hollywood*.

And it's far more pressing and critical than the angst and quasi-parental concerns these weird choices engender in us grown-ups. I can deal with all the questionable choices that many young people are making today because I'm relatively sure that we all made similar (or much worse, but probably less long-lasting) choices in our youth and yet, amazingly enough, we're still here, standing tall, and giving them advice and the "benefit" of our wisdom – such as it is.

But I'm not talking about something that's a preference or an option that we can take or leave – I'm talking about a problem that threatens to undermine something so fundamental and basic to the conduct of business (and especially to early-stage angel investing) that almost everyone (other than those in the film or music business) has always taken it for gospel and for granted. They say every day in the film business, "I'll love you 'til I don't" so get used to it. But that kind of fleeting attachment or commitment and the complete absence of sincerity that's "just business" in those worlds isn't the way we hope and expect that the rest of the sane (and square) business world conducts itself.

That's why I'm getting increasingly concerned about this very basic idea. I recently heard Alan Matthew (a long-time successful options and commodities trader) express it forcefully in about 15 different ways throughout a recent talk he gave to several hundred entrepreneurs at 1871. He said that, in every deal he does, and in every transaction: "My word is my bond." And it's just that simple – especially in the trading pits in Chicago – where the entire ecosystem depends on trust and the ability for everyone to rely on the commitments and honesty of the other players. But the problem is that - even as essential a part as this attitude is to how we do business in Chicago - I don't think we're doing a good job of communicating this very critical concept to today's young entrepreneurs. Too many of them live in a different conceptual world – one driven by situational ethics. And it sucks.

Telling people half the story or what they want to hear instead of what they need to hear isn't a funding solution – it's an invitation to a later slaughter. And it's usually the entrepreneur and the management team who will ultimately get killed. So it makes sense to share ALL of the news all the time – if for no other reason than to just save yourself all the grief coming down the line. The truth never hurts unless it ought to and sometimes it's a powerful wake-up call for all concerned. There's never a really good or special time to decide to tell the truth – the time is all the time.

But, if you haven't been there (to make the right choice regardless of how hard or discouraging it may be or how it may impact your financing or prospects) and there's no one more experienced around to guide you because you're running full-speed ahead and you're also making it up as you go, it's far too easy to take a quick slide down that slippery ethical slope. And once you lose someone's confidence, once they come to believe that you don't share and abide by their fundamental values, you will never get their trust and support entirely back.

And, honestly, because a whole generation of kids have been told (at least since second grade) that they're amazing, exceptional and completely unique, it's just a short step for them to conclude that the ordinary rules don't apply to them and that morals are just for little people and that they're way above that somewhat mundane conformity and far too smart for it as well. An old friend of mine used to say – by way of excusing virtually anything disgusting that he managed to do - that exceptional people deserve special concessions. I'm afraid his disease may be spreading.

As I often kiddingly say when I'm talking about building your company's culture and instilling critical values in your people and your business processes: "These are my principles. If you don't like them, I have others." But that's always intended as a joke because – in the real world – we don't get to pick and choose when to honor our promises and commitments. We say what we'll do and then we do what we said we'd do. It couldn't be more straightforward – you don't get to be truthful some of the time or some time later or when it's a better or more convenient time. The truth doesn't vary based on circumstances.

And frankly, I'm not even sure that, in some cases, this is purely an issue of intentional dishonesty or immorality. I think it's just as much a lack of experience and education combined with way too much enthusiasm. Entrepreneurs can talk themselves into anything (I call this the "that hooker really liked me" condition) and, once they do, they want to sell it to the world. But whenever you find that you're having to shade the truth or forget some ugly facts in order to convince yourself or talk your team or some investor into something that you're not even sure you yourself buy off on, you're probably not doing yourself or anyone else a favor. It's almost inevitably a bad deal which you should back away from as quickly as possible.

And, while it's great to be highly motivated, it's not even a little cool if no one trusts your motives. It takes a time and hard work to build any kind of relationship, but just an instant and a suspicion (a long way from proof) to destroy it. And I know just how hard it is to say things that no one wants to hear, but that's part of the leader's job – it's not delegable and it's not optional.

It takes a great deal of experience and a whole bunch of broken dreams and busted relationships to appreciate that to be trusted is a much greater compliment than to be loved. Entrepreneurs – without a doubt – need and want (first and foremost) to be loved. It's part of the sickness which drives us. But, at the end of the day, trust is the only thing that you can really take to the bank.

WHY RABBITS DON'T RUN
BIG BUSINESSES

I've always been partial to Thumper's Dad's advice about communication. In case you don't recall it from the *Bambi* movie, his Dad said: "If you can't say something nice, don't say nothin' at all" - at least as Thumper recalled it. And, as it happens, this is pretty good advice for small talking animals, but it's a really bad way to run your company. You can't build a successful business based on a culture that values quiet, courtesy and consensus over honest conversations, constructive criticism and confrontations where necessary. Politely keeping the peace can't ever trump telling the truth. The best operators know two things for certain: (1) the truth only hurts when you don't tell it and (2) the truth only hurts when it should. I realize that sometimes it's very hard to tell the truth, but it's just as hard to hide it and a whole lot less productive.

White lies and other pleasantries are worthless – they're a lot like eating junk food – you get a temporary lift, but no nourishment; the problem persists; the emptiness returns; and nothing gets done in the meantime. And when you encourage people to lie even a little, you learn quickly that people who will lie for you will eventually lie to you. Better a few bruises and battered egos than a bankrupt business based on bullshitting each other. And honestly, it's just so much easier for everyone because when you always tell the truth, you never have to waste time and energy trying to remember your lies.

Frankly, an aggressive culture where people stand their ground and argue their cases makes for much better ultimate decisions as long as people are arguing for the right reasons. The right reasons are to get to the truth and the best results for the business and not because people need to be right and won't shut up until they grind everyone down and wear everyone else out. Make your point; say your piece; and sit your butt down. Don't argue with the truth.

You want your people to fearlessly face the facts. As one of the great old Hollywood moguls used to say: "I want my people to tell me the truth even if it costs them their jobs". But seriously, unpleasant facts don't fade away when you ignore them – they fester – and refusing to look at them won't change the situation or improve things until you do something about them. Facts may change, but the truth never does. And waiting only makes things worse. It's a funny thing about the truth – the truth doesn't have a time of its own. There's never a better or best time to tell someone the truth – the time for truth is always <u>now</u>.

I think all of the foregoing comes down to a few simple "rules" which you need to share (somewhat obsessively) with all of your people (not just newbies in orientations) on a regular and recurring basis. My suggested and very basic rules are as follows:

(1) Tell the Truth

No shades, no strokes, no "smoothing" the news or softening the blows – give it to me simple and straight. Figures don't lie, but they often don't tell the whole story. Make sure that the metrics don't get in the way of a clear message. As they say, everyone is entitled to their own opinion, but the facts are the facts – you don't get to pick and choose them.

(2) Tell It Timely

Nothing ugly really improves over time. Don't wait to bring me bad news. The sooner and shorter the better. I need a brief, not as book. Nothing elaborate – just accurate information delivered on time and in time.

(3) Tell Everyone

Don't assume that everyone else (or anyone else) necessarily knows what you know. Spread the word. In addition to the general virtues of transparency and making sure that eventually the message does get thru to the right people; going wide makes it more likely that meaningful and actionable information will also get to people who need whether you even realize that or not.

(4) Tell It 'til Someone Listens

I don't think that, in most businesses, you can <u>ever</u> over-communicate relevant and time-sensitive data. But you will often encounter people who fall into two problem piles: (a) people who don't want to say what nobody wants to hear; and (b) people who don't want to hear what needs to and has to be said and spread throughout the organization. These folks are master manipulators and they typically follow the standard three-step routine in dealing with "inconvenient", but sadly true facts: (i) first they aggressively ridicule; (ii) then they violently resist; and finally (iii) they get with the program – claim that they knew it all along – and treat things as obvious and self-evident.   You need to keep spreading the word until you're sure that you've done as much as you can reasonably do to let the folks in charge know what you know. If they don't listen after that, so be it. It's frustrating and depressing, but in many businesses, it's a fact of life. As Bruce Springsteen says: "When the truth is spoken and it makes no difference – something in your heart goes cold". After a while, if it's clear that you're wasting your breath, find a better place to be.

(5) Tell It All the Time

And finally, truth-telling is not a sometime thing. As with everything else that matters in your business, it's an everyday, all day part of creating and maintaining an environment where the organization learns and grows and where things continue to improve through a constant iterative process. You can't make innovation through iteration work if you don't have a constant and accurate flow of data telling you what's working and what's not and where you're going wrong.

TELL A SIMPLE STORY

Almost every day I meet and speak with young entrepreneurs trying to get their new businesses off the ground. I don't generally have a lot of time, but I always try to give anyone at least a few minutes to explain what they're trying to do and then I can decide very quickly whether it makes more sense to meet further with them. Frankly, what you can't basically say in ten minutes about your business or your idea really isn't worth saying. I don't think of these little chats as "pitches" (elevator or otherwise) – they're much more like speed dates where you're trying to decide very quickly whether what you're hearing makes sense; whether there's a real business or opportunity lurking there; and whether the person you're speaking to has the passion, enthusiasm and smarts to turn a good idea into a real business.

After 50 years of doing this, I can tell you that it's actually possible to make these initial decisions with a high degree of accuracy in a matter of minutes. Now I admit that I will definitely miss out on a few real opportunities and turn down or not pursue some very talented people, but, by and large – especially since we're all dealing with limited time and scarce resources – the system works and works pretty well.

And here's the main reason why – it's not that I'm so perceptive and smart; it's that way too many people make it too easy to turn them down because they're so unprepared to take their best shot in the moment when the opportunity is there and because they don't really understand how to make the most of that short window of time.

As we used to say in the music industry, it's really easy to tell when a song is bad, but only the public and the market will ultimately decide what sells. Note that I said "what sells", not necessarily what's good. The music business today is all about selling disks and downloads, not making great music. Always has been; always will be.

And it's the same story with describing new businesses. If you're all over the place; if you're trying to be all things to too many people; if your story is so complicated that it's hard to even follow; or if you've got a solution in search of a problem, it's going to be pretty easy to say "thanks, but no thanks". You've got one shot, one moment, and one opportunity to get right to the heart of the matter and the most crucial part of the entire process is to tell a simple story.

How simple? Your story should answer 3 simple questions about your company which, by the way, are the very same questions that will inform and guide your company for its entire existence. These answers are also every bit as significant for each and every employee as they are for any investors. So it's pretty important to get the answers right at the outset. The answers might change over time, but the fundamental questions never do.

Here they are:

Who are We?

Management and team members' <u>relevant</u> experience and credentials

Where are We Going?

Short and long term objectives and goals – abbreviated milestones – timeframe

Why?

What problem is being addressed and solved – time, money, productivity, status

Short, sweet and to the point. You've got to be a ruthless editor and there's no question that the hardest choices are about what to leave out, not what to include. You need to think of both detail and elaboration as forms of pollution. Cut to the quick. And stick to your story.

One of the nastiest things venture guys like to do to "newbies" is to ask them how big their businesses can be and how many opportunities and directions there are to grow the businesses. And when they charge off into the future and start building their castles in the sky; the VCs look at each other, roll their eyes, and say to themselves: "Boy, this guy's not focused at all."

It's an old but important trick from debate class – tell the story you need to tell, be relentless, stay on point, keep it short, and make the limited time that you have count. Everything else can come later. Bottom line: tell a simple story.

BE A ROLE PLAYER OR ROLL
YOUR OWN?

There's a lot of conversation these days about being an entrepreneur and starting your own business and it's very reminiscent of the early dotcom days when everyone thought they'd spend a few dollars, quickly build a website, and just wait for the bucks to start rolling in. Everyone knows how well that worked out for the lion's share of the companies, but many young people today haven't taken the inescapable lessons of those frothy times to heart. They think that starting a business is like learning to swim the hard way – you jump (or a helpful parent or older sibling tosses you) into the deep end of the pool - and everyone (except maybe your older brother) hopes you quickly figure things out and that you don't drown. To put this vignette into the proper perspective, the end of this particular fantasy would be that you'd swim a couple of lengths and then emerge as a slightly better swimmer than Michael Phelps.

In addition, there's another strain of embarrassing arrogance floating around the West Coast where the "Y" guys maintain that they can identify a good, young and talented team of guys with a mediocre idea and then, by magic and the massive application of money, their "expertise", and their network connections, invent a new and better business for the team to build. This is, by and large, utter BS and the few pivots and successful examples that have worked out shouldn't mislead the vast majority of us into thinking that this approach makes the slightest sense. Your idea may change over time and, in many cases, it will have to, but at least it's your idea. If you're plowing someone else's field or chasing another man's dream, at the end of the day, you're just a hired hand. So stick with making your own best ideas real – this startup stuff is just too hard to be doing for someone else. And I get that everyone's dream these days is to be working for themselves building an exciting new business. That's where we'd all like to end up, but that's not where the journey starts.

I spoke recently to a young man who said that he had decided that he really wants to work for a technology startup. I, myself, would like to grow at least 10 inches and play center for the Celtics. I'd say we have about the same long-term prospects because just wanting doesn't make anything so. It's good to have desire, but the details don't take care of themselves. Passion needs to be melded with preparation and planning. A goal without a concrete plan to get there is just a daydream or a delusion. Your plan doesn't have to be the world's greatest anything. It doesn't have to be complete; it doesn't have to be perfect; and it's going to change a million times along the way, but it's a place to start. As we used to say in the movie business, "the screenplay isn't the movie that finally gets made, but it's what gets the movie made."

And, as many times as I have said that an entrepreneur's ignorance can be a competitive advantage in some respects, the truth is that you don't get into this crazy game simply by knocking on a business's front door and asking nicely. If wishes were fishes, every boy would be driving a Porsche. But hope alone is not a strategy for success.

And that's why, when I was asked the question about whether it's better at the outset to be a founder or to work for a startup and learn the ropes, it wasn't even a close question. The odds of achieving some ultimate happiness and financial success are at least 1000% better if you take the time to learn your craft and develop a valuable set of skills in some area that interests you and where you've got some aptitude. After that, the sky really is the only limit.

So plan to be a great employee and to grow into an important role player first and build your future path and your next plan from there instead of from nowhere. Just one note of caution – try to work for someone who can actually teach you something of actual value – not a person who's been doing things the same way forever or someone who's 15 minutes older than you and learning the job as he or she goes. Also it's a really good idea to try to work for someone who has fewer emotional and mental problems than you have.

So that's job number one – get started, start learning, and go from there. Then, and only then, can you start thinking about your next step. Just like Cinderella, if you want to get a great job at a great company, you've got to bring something to the Ball. You'll need the skills you developed in the jobs you've had before (not anything you learned in school) along with a killer work ethic as well as unbelievable persistence. With that kind of package, you're actually worth hiring.

COULD IT BE MAGIC?

I t's National Magic Week. I've been a "professional" magician since I was about 9 years old and I firmly believe that nothing in my training or background (except my mother's raising me to have a level of ridiculous confidence which was utterly disproportionate to my actual looks and abilities) has had a greater impact on my success as an entrepreneur than practicing magic for my peers and their parents. Every prospective entrepreneur should have to learn to perform and "sell" a dozen tricks to an unruly crowd. The lessons learned are good for a lifetime.

Frankly, the kids in the birthday party audience were always easy to control and to fool...the parents (especially those paying me to perform) not so much. They always insisted on seeing how the tricks were done and, as everyone knows, a good magician never tells. Managing the adults and telling them "No" was a learning experience that was at least as valuable as learning how to deal from the bottom of the deck or to pull a sickly little rabbit from a hat.

And the truth is that - as much as people ask you for the explanation or to "tell them the truth" - they actually all prefer the magic of the illusion to knowing how the effect was accomplished. They just don't realize it until it's too late. Because once we know how the trick was done, it loses all its power to amaze, inspire and confound us. No one really wants to see how the sausage was made.

If this is starting to sound a little like an entrepreneur's daily journey; it's not a coincidence. Selling yourself and your team and your investors on your dream every day is itself a magical act. Starting a new business is a triumph of imagination over intelligence and passion over experience. Because – as I always say – if any of us knew how long and hard the actual process was going to be, we probably would never have started down the path in the first place.

Startups have a great deal in common with magic.

First, they involve masterful storytelling. When you look closely at a magician's performance, you realize that the power and the passion is in the dramatic way that the trick is explained and the story is told. The effect (the action) is just a technical process which is more about engineering than emotion. Capturing and conveying that excitement and enthusiasm is what the best entrepreneurs do every day.

Second, they involve the willful suspension of disbelief – at least for a while. We don't believe for a minute that the woman is going to be chopped in half, but we go along with the gag and the guillotine and our hearts race all the same as the blade descends. Setting off to change an industry, invent a new way of doing things, save thousands of lives, etc. isn't something that happens every day, but these things will never happen if we don't believe that they can and try to turn those dreams into realities. Feasibility will compromise us all in the end, but we have to believe in our dreams – however impossible they may seem – and never let the turkeys get us down.

And finally, we are blessed to be living in an age of amazing new technologies available to millions of people across the world. The truth is that any sufficiently advanced technology is basically indistinguishable from magic anyway. If we continue to create and capture the multitude of opportunities out there today to combine our vibrant imaginations with our powerful new technologies, we can all be magicians in our own right. If you can dream it, you can do it. Because, as they say at Disney, the magic's the magic within you.

ABOUT THE AUTHOR

Howard Tullman is the CEO of 1871 in Chicago where digital startups get their start. He is also the General Managing Partner of two venture funds: Chicago High-Tech Investment Partners and G2T3V, LLC, which both focus on funding disruptive innovators. He is the former Chairman and CEO of Tribeca Flashpoint Media Arts Academy in Chicago. He is an active member of numerous city, state and civic boards and organizations and a tireless supporter and mentor to many start-ups and other businesses and individuals. He has successfully founded more than a dozen high-tech businesses in his 50 year career and created more than $1 billion in investor value as well as thousands of new jobs. He writes a regular weekly blog on The Perspiration Principles for Inc. Magazine and can be directly contacted:

- by email at h@1871.com
- on twitter @tullman
- his blog: tullman.blogspot.com
- his primary website: www.tullman.com

To get all of Howard's blog posts in one download, visit Blogintobook.com/tullman/.